YOUTUBE MILLIONAIRE MASTERY

The Agency & Consultant's Guide to 7-Figure Success

Stewart Vickers

Serpply Ltd

Copyright © 2024 Stewart Vickers

All rights reserved

The characters and events portrayed in this book are fictitious. Any similarity to real persons, living or dead, is coincidental and not intended by the author.

No part of this book may be reproduced, or stored in a retrieval system, or transmitted in any form or by any means, electronic, mechanical, photocopying, recording, or otherwise, without express written permission of the publisher.

*For Yoshi who's 1200 views in 24 hours motivated me to try something new.
For Craig as a generous mentor,
and Julian as a worthy competitor.*

CONTENTS

Title Page
Copyright
Dedication
Preface
My Business Was Doomed
Imperfection drives engagement.
The decision to go public
Network = Net Worth
The Real Money
Technical set up
Video Ideas
Scripting
Hook and Title
Call To Action
Lead Magnets
Descriptions
Thumbnails
Emailing your list
Advanced Engagement
Selling To Your List
Volume and Consistency

Monetisation
Closing Thoughts

PREFACE

Books are a fantastic source of knowledge. Personally I have always wanted to be an author and still enjoy the authority of having my name on a cover.

But for a subject like video marketing certain topics really don't translate into the written word well.

I wrote this book to accompany a much more comprehensive video course on everything I did and continue to do to blow my agency up to seven figures in about six months.

While this book really goes into great detail on every step of my process, and in its own right covers some of my deeper thought processes which are difficult to express on camera, I strongly encourage you to try the course as well.

It is packed full of over-the-shoulder tutorials and live case studies where I record myself recording my videos and all the planning and theory I do before and after.

I continue adding to the course with all my latest findings and developments and therefore it will never be at a lower price than today.

To make this a real no-brainer for you the course comes with a 30-day moneyback guarantee.

Go to: https://seojesus.com/youtube-course/ or scan the QR code below.

MY BUSINESS WAS DOOMED

My 26th birthday was a disaster.

My relationship with my then partner had been falling apart for months. Traditionally we would share a celebration with my close friend and lodger as we all had birthdays within the same two weeks.

But while previously I had got a great turnout for my share of the invitations, this time I was told to keep it minimal.

Normally I am, firstly, the kind of people person who enjoys going out, making connections and calling even the slightest acquaintance a "friend".

And secondly, I am a marketer who knows that - for 100 invitations with a medium so passive as Facebook with the lead quality I have just described - about 30 might actually turn up.

My partner and lodger on the other hand wouldn't invite more than capacity and so previously were left with a poor turnout. Hence my restriction this time.

At the time I was travelling the world building my business and getting my first clients for my SEO agency, so couldn't be bothered to argue over message.

I remember it exactly - in a Prague AirBnB in between a metal festival and a digital marketing conference - knowing that as August progressed we were getting ever closer to the end of September when the three dates fell.

Sure enough my own share of the party was minimal while plus ones of plus ones filled my house, trampled my garden, and I found an interesting situation of three acquaintances in my bed - but soon enough for them to still be fully clothed.

The Prague conference had also not been impressive. Appropriately enough, despite being described as a digital marketing conference with representation from finance, gambling, supplements and adult, they had rather underplayed the significance of adult. It was, in fact, a total porn conference.

But that was exactly how I had built my business. Within six months of quitting my day job I had a six figure agency fuelled purely from in person events.

From local networks to private masterminds, I had travelled the world hard. First I was at a digital nomad conference in London where someone told me about a high ticket mastermind in Medellin Colombia.

After a rather fanciful filling in of the application (sure, I make six figures…) I was accepted

The ticket price was scary, never mind last minute flights across the world, but I knew that with 20 people paying that kind of fee I was very likely to get a client worth ten times that.

This was a great experience with two days in the conference hotel and then two days white water rafting in the rainforest, including a camp all set up for us and helicopters to get back. Even if I didn't get clients I was having a hell of a good time.

This had all been bankrolled by a website I had sold, a side hustle I had nurtured over two years. Building my agency was the best use of those funds I could think of - and high level in-person events seemed a much better risk-reward profile than blowing the load on paid ads.

It took a while but it worked. A few months after Medellin someone I really connected with signed up with me.

Then there was Prague, which wasn't so successful but remains one of my favourite stories to share. If nothing else, I got close to some of the top names in may industry (they didn't know the conference's specialism either).

Then I spoke in Utrecht at a very small event for 16 people. One of them signed up. Sadly this was an early learning about the value of lead qualification and managing expectations as they cancelled after one month having expected far more in so little time. But it covered the cost of the trip.

And landing sleep-deprived in Bangkok in October I had a message from someone at the first London event. They too were now ready to get on board.

And so this continued. I figured this one strategy was good enough for now.

But into 2023 there remained that creeping anxiety that if I can only sell from in-person, I had to keep back enough money to get back out and find a client in the unlikely but plausible event that all my clients suddenly cancelled.

Those first events were probably costing me around 3000 - 4000 dollars each. You don't get that quality of lead by going to your local chamber of commerce with the high street accountants and estate agents. These were international flights, high ticket events at nice hotels and VIP dinners for that extra face time with big personal brands.

Despite growing steadily I was also burning that cash pile from the website.

As much as I enjoyed the travel, a client cancelling meant repeating the effort - preferably twice to make up the loss and get back to growth.

And there were always the duds. Not just Prague, but other events where the right client just wasn't in the room.

If the market took a turn for the worst and everyone cancelled - there was no guarantee I could spend another 4k, get to an event, connect with someone who resonated with me and have them sign up within a short timeframe.

And I started getting a lot more duds. Dubai, Mexico City, Lisbon, Spain and a VIP treatment in London. Each of these I had branched out to bigger events in broader industries. And while I had learned lots and made great connections with each, none had yielded any actual cash in the bank.

Not only does this stall growth and present a big risk if clients start cancelling, but your vulnerability in such a situation can destroy your business. Good business is all about boundaries. And I'm pretty terrible at that.

Just as a strong romantic relationship should leave both partners free to walk away at any point - and instead choose to stay together - business relationships are the same.

You should know your price and stick with it to avoid devaluing your service.

You should stick to your key deliverables rather than saying yes to a load of requests that stress out you and your team, destroy your margin and annoy your client when it's done poorly. Or have the client come back with even more requests after.

And you shouldn't take on any clients you don't think is a good fit.

But in a situation where you're not confident in your ability to replace clients easily, you inevitably end up failing all of these. Reducing prices, making excessive promises and taking on clients who will drain your energy and your wallet.

I'm grateful that while this was a possibility for me I never reached a situation where that was necessary. We maintained good service, kept to a relatively clean set of deliverables and didn't take on any nightmare clients. But I was still pretty broke.

Throughout the summer of 2023 I worked hard to fix this problem. I wrote my first book The Power Lever Method and invested heavily in growing my personal brand.

I even hired someone to run a podcast for me to interview these high level people and then refer them to me as an apparently unbiased recommendation: "You mentioned you struggle with marketing? I know this great guy you should meet. He DEFINITELY doesn't own this podcast or anything…"

I created directories so that clients could pay to feature on my page ranking on Google for their target market, so I could then upsell them and have me rank their website for the same market.

I spent thousands of dollars on Facebook ads, paying an attractive model to recite a number of scripts I had crafted from classic copywriting formulas with different hooks to test out.

Nothing was working.

I had one good lead from Facebook. We had a good call and he agreed to come on board, but had a few invoices to pay in the meantime and so asked if he could sign up next week.

Of course, despite multiple follow ups on different platforms, I never heard from him again.

My 27th birthday was a vast improvement. My new partner had moved in and my lodger had moved out. I had cut down drinking significantly that year and decided that rather than a hedonistic night of 50 drinking buddies I would have just a small circle of intimate friends - each invited by direct message rather than a mass Facebook event. And it was wonderful.

That Monday morning I unfolded my laptop and opened my worst business nightmare.

One good client had been looking that their cashflow and needed to cut spend for a few months. No big deal.

But then that afternoon I got a message from the Medellin client. They had seen great results. I had taken their traffic from 300 visitors per month to more than 1000, all for relevant queries. But somehow it just wasn't converting. Somehow none of this large volume of people were sold on the product. I regard this client as a good personal friend despite living on separate continents and he explained to me about some very expensive medical treatment he was having, and so reluctantly he had no choice but to cancel.

Now things are getting uncomfortable. My monthly recurring revenue had been flat for nearly six months. But there was no change to the plan. The renowned copywriter Dan Kennedy has a quote I love : when things are good, double down on sales and marketing. When things are bad, double down on sales and marketing.

There really was no difference in my priorities before these clients left and after. Just get more clients.

Then on the Wednesday I got a voice note on WhatsApp. It was my highest paying client.

They explained how they valued my work and how thankful they were to have found me. But their son has a bit of SEO experience and is offering - quite persistently - to do their's for free.

Each of these clients had been quite happy with the service with no complaints. But I had lost half my revenue in just three days.

I told the team and explained that as it stood there shouldn't be any need for cutting back on staff. But we had to do all we could to save costs and keep our current clients.

I felt that kind of numbness where you just find the situation hilarious. It was after all quite expected as a scenario I dreaded. And I was still up compared to where I was a year before - although I had a lot more cash in the bank back then.

But my proud story of reaching six figures in six months was over.

For about two weeks.

And one month later I hit an all time high.

It was the Sunday after the painful week that I received an email from someone saying they had watched my Youtube videos and were interested in becoming my client.

This was just three weeks after I had started publishing on Youtube. Like many entrepreneurs, I had been meaning to get around to Youtube for years but constantly hesitated on the set up: the right camera, microphone, software or editor.

But recently I had heard about the power of simple screen shares.

So I did exactly that. Basic laptop webcam and microphone. Recording with the Loom chrome extension.

My first video got more than 10,000 views. To reinforce the "done is better than perfect mantra" I had even exported the wrong video quality and given these viewers a blurry 480p version of a complex process with lots of text.

But most didn't care. The content was good. It was about how I published 500 AI blog posts which had actually started ranking on Google and getting traffic.

How I rank 500+ Instant AI
Blog Posts on Google In 3...

12K views • 8 months ago 8x

And those who did care - and commented such witticisms as "was it recorded on a Casio calculator" - simply fuelled more engagement on the video and got it to blow up more.

That imperfect action message I had got from one of my clients when they were speaking at an event. They had found that after publishing a "6 tips to…" video which inadvertently had only 5 tips the rage that ensued helped the video to trend on Youtube.

IMPERFECTION DRIVES ENGAGEMENT.

You can weaponise internet trolls for your own gain.

The last 10 years has seen the rise of plenty of controversial figures who have provoked polarised audiences for exactly this result. If you can start a war in your comments section, then you have struck gold.

But I, coming from the world of SEO and manipulating algorithms by any means necessary, had also found a way to drive even pretty basic videos of nerdy SEO tutorials to trend on Youtube through a mix of clever processes.

The crazy thing was I was still very early stage in my channel when someone reached out to buy from me.

I was still trying to promote my marketing services for coaches, but here was someone who had landed on my personal brand website, found my email and reached out to me directly.

And it started happening again and again.

Within about three weeks I went from losing half my revenue to closing about two new clients per week.

Plus, getting on these calls was remarkable. The prospect would come onto Zoom wide-eyed. "My God, it's really you!" They would tell me how they've been watching my content for weeks - recalling individual things I had said.

They looked at me like I looked at my industry celebrities who I had listened to on hours of podcasts on my daily commute to my day job years before.

These prospects were pre-sold. They had already come to trust me, and had gone out of their way to track me down and find my email address.
Often seeing a lot more of my personal branding in the process.

They didn't even fit my "SEO for coaches" title and they didn't care - they had seen my skill and wanted to know what it would take to work with me.

This was entirely un-optimised. Crude rudimentary videos that inspired people to find me and email me. From then on I knew what I had to do and quickly started rebuilding my brand for this new successful angle.

Gone was The Power Lever Method of SEO For Coaches and here was SEO Jesus, with his free lead magnet of the Ranking Revelations newsletter - to which people replied full of heartfelt praise that I delivered more value than any of the other YouTubers in my industry.

Top names in my industry started reaching out. One even asked to be on my podcast - when I didn't actually have a podcast.

I had gone from long haul flights to hang out with 20 possible prospects for $4000 to spending an hour a day recording and publishing a Youtube video that would be seen by thousands of eager leads.

When I went to an SEO conference in Thailand that November, still just weeks after my first video, I was recognised as SEO Jesus repeatedly, asked for selfies and more. Amongst a small world of geeks I had become an icon. Plenty of them are broke, but plenty of them are not.

Now make no mistake, this was not an overnight success. I had been publishing daily. I was trawling through my back catalogue of years of SEO experience to come up with interesting case studies and then reframing them with a hook that I knew was capable of trending - typically "how I achieved [dream outcome] in no time and with no budget".

Then the follow-up after a video was important with a set of processes to get as much engagement on that video as possible to make it rank.

Youtube wants you to succeed. It gets a big share of your ad revenue and wants to keep people engaged on its platform consuming content. Therefore it is always looking for the next big thing.

As soon as your video goes live it is under scrutiny.

Now of course Youtube can't algorithmically watch your video and decide if it is good content or not.

Like Google, it relies on user signals. And it wants to know if your video could go viral. Therefore those first few hours are crucial to get people clicking, watching, liking, commenting, subscribing so that Youtube is inspired to max out your video across the platform to fully utilise the asset you have given it.

Do this right and you'll end up recommended on the homepage, related videos and more.

In this book I'm going to give you the method I used to succeed on Youtube. And when I say succeed, I mean going from burnt out and broke to being a celebrity of my industry in just three months. I'm talking about opening up multiple revenue streams - from banner ad revenue, to affiliate, to services and sponsorships.

Like so many other businesses, my message remains the same: take action and be persistent. These are almost certainly the only factors that decide whether you succeed or fail.

THE DECISION TO GO PUBLIC

Hesitations affect everything. We know this all too well.

I mentioned how great my partner is; I could have missed her altogether. We were in pretty separate walks of life - no mutual friends or venues. But I decided to go to a club night that wasn't in my usual repertoire.

I saw her on the dance floor and took a further unusual step for me of enthusiastically dancing.

Having overcome both those potential pitfalls, she walked away.

I panicked that after all the build up I had missed my chance. So I sped after her and clumsily spoke to her. The rest is history.

Imperfect action is paramount. I cannot understate how many great things have been missed through perfectionism or hesitation of waiting for the right moment. And I say that frustratingly to myself as a fairly shy person.

But shyness is easily the main reason people don't get on camera and get on Youtube.

Plus there is the very real threat of internet trolls and the like.

But the fact is if you can overcome this then that is a huge advantage because so few do.

I always liked the "build to sell" ideology, that is to avoid becoming the face of the company. Run the company as a true asset with a team of experts in their respective specialisms. You are the business owner and not the manager. You work on the business and not in the business.

But the fact is in a competitive landscape your personal brand is one of your strongest assets.

When I was flying back from Medellin I messed up. Having been burning my remaining Pesos in the bar on very cheap pints I got to my gate to find I had completely missed the ESTA requirement for transit through the USA.
I filled it in at the gate but the approval came through minutes after the gate had closed. Feeling the financial pinch of buying a new flight, a started emailing potential referral contacts. It's amazing how all the methods of sales and marketing you've been told become much easier to implement when you're under pressure. Someone had a lead for me who seemed a great fit.

But they pushed back on the grounds that they were going with another big name in the industry - because of the trust they had in his brand.

This brand was enough to beat a personal recommendation from someone this person had actually worked with.

There are studies which show the more time you spend with a client the more likely they are to buy.

It's no wonder my initial success was fuelled by having dinner and drinks with people over several days.

If I had sent a cold email or LinkedIn message to these same people I very much doubt they would have been interested.

This is why webinars have become so popular as you are put live in a room with someone for an hour in which they give you loads of content on the outcomes they can provide and only reveal the price at the very end after you have been fully brainwashed.

When someone sees me on Youtube they will get a very quick "vibe" as to whether the like me or not. This is human nature and applies to every interaction we ever have.

And this is perhaps the most important point. It is absolutely fine if they don't. It sometimes gives me a strange feeling when I think individual videos have been seen 10,000 times - my face, my home, my laptop screen. But it is absolutely fine.

You are ultimately talking to the extreme minority who are your ideal clients. No one else is going to buy from them and you owe them nothing. I get complaints about selling things. Of giving bad information. Of not telling them what they wanted which is how can they do something without working hard for it.

The fact is I know in my mind that I am making an effort churning out a video every day of valuable information. The power dynamic is very much the other way round.

Probably the worst comment I ever had was of a tutting sound I sometimes make between sentences as a natural public speaking nervous twitch and someone said please stop making that sound. My response was simple - don't watch my videos then.

I repeat my earlier point that you should use negative feedback to your advantage. Yes it takes strength. And yes it's going to happen. But if lowlifes want to waste their time commenting on your video all they are doing is helping your video to trend.

Hopefully you'll get a decent following of supporters too who will pile in and fight the trolls on your behalf and again feed the algorithm.

It may sound shallow but really keep your eye on the money. You may feel uncomfortable being on camera. But would that discomfort feel worthwhile if you knew you would get a $10,000 client from that video?

I come on to the subject of volume and ad revenue later but this is worth stating early on. Do not get caught up in the belief that your videos need to reach thousands. It's a double-edged sword. You feel put off that you have to grind your way up to that level while your videos are only getting 60 views, while you're not even motivated to get there because having 60,000 people watching your video seems scary.

In this book we are not talking about volume and ad revenue - although they are definitely helpful. We are talking about growing a relatively small channel to target the right high ticket clients. Often when I get on sales calls the prospect will mention the videos that really spoke to them and they are often the quieter uploads with less than 1000 views.

From dropping below $10,000 per month in September I hit $25,000 per month by the end of the year with just 5000 Youtube subscribers.

By February we hit $55,000 and - even better - managed to maintain that figure.

In that time I qualified for monetisation - the prize of many aspiring Youtubers - but made no more than $200 on ads in that same period.

So I challenge you to put yourself on camera and be vulnerable.

You'll be doing something most of your competitors aren't. If you can follow that up with then presenting great content and being likeable to a small minority of people then you will have a killer lead generation strategy.

Should this be a step too far for you then there are alternatives. Depending on your offer you can of course do a screen share that does not include your face. If you want a further degree of separation then you can even use AI voices - or go as far as the new emerging trend of AI avatars. But I discourage this. Keep it simple and go with your own vulnerable, powerful self.

As for the build to sell methodology I'm sure my numbers have already made it quite clear that it's better to make money and be the face of the brand than hide in the shadows and starve.

But truthfully I feel quite confident in being the influencer promoting my brands. I'm currently building up my following as an SEO expert and driving leads for my link building agency.

Agencies only sell realistically for 3 - 4 x their monthly profit anyway, and usually struggle to make a profit margin greater than 40%, and so are much more appealing as cash flow businesses. That cash flow can then be invested into better more liquid assets.

But hypothetically if I were to sell there could be all manner of contracts where I keep promoting the service in videos, or simply sell it on the basis on its current client list.

I have friends who are still the "face" of their agencies they sold years before. That following I'm building on my channel will be my core audience for all kinds of other projects, often very separate entities to myself. Plus I've had all manner of affiliate opportunities come my way offering me special rates for recommending them.

With many agencies only making a margin of 20 - 30% it's no surprise many business influencers either white label or recommend a partner service for a 20% commission and none of the work.

Oh, remember that referral lead I lost to big name in my industry because of their brand and trust? That brand was a white label. Building the following and being the spokesperson sadly seems to matter far more than what you're actually selling.

NETWORK = NET WORTH

I get very tired of this phrase.

I'm tired of conferences.

After two years of almost constant travel for the business I was worn out. Most of the events I ended up at were the same.

Foggy-eyed beginners either eagerly awaiting their big jump from the corporate world but clinging anxiously on (I was exactly the same), or recent jumpers who had gained some early successes and were convinced they had it made.

But quite quickly you start to find that most of these events were a fascade. Mindset talks all about the power of belief, while giving little in terms of actionable steps to a crowd fighting to make six figures a year.

That sounds great early on, but soon you realise six figures is really not much to shout about. Lawyers, doctors and a whole host of other professions make six figures with the security of an employment contract. They don't have to market themselves, pay staff or do many of the pitfalls of entrepreneurship while balancing the fact that business could simply dry up in a few years. That course or coaching program driving their revenue could be largely irrelevant in six months.

And within these conferences you inevitably find a Ponzi-like mix of masterminds, events, networks and communities.

I don't really buy the mantra of "those who can't, teach" but I've seen plenty of opportunists attempting to monetize networks this way.

"You should join my community, you'll get clients out of it!"

"Come to my event! You'll get lots of clients."

Or the worst I've had. A sales call with a "business leader" who, after receiving my full recommendations and $2000 per month proposal, asked if I would be up for a "collaboration" where she gets the work for free and I get to present to her community.

"Who is in the community? What kind of demographic are we talking about?" I asked, knowing that with my costs the $2000 per month proposal would cost Around $1300 per month to provide.

"Entrepreneurs and business owners" she said. Which I interpreted as yet more well-meaning but financially-stretched hustlers who were sold the dream of joining this community to get their own clients.

This may well be a bit of a rant. But I distinctly dislike the idea of "network" as a verb. At a conference you talk to people and have coffee or beers, as real humans.

"I'm going to network for a bit" to me just sounds reductive, that I am mingling for purely commercial gain.

On the flip side, I have been to really high level conferences in the past with the celebrities of my niche.

Some of them I got on with well and received great mentorship from.

But plenty didn't talk to me. They barely even looked at me or regarded my existence.

Why would they?

As experienced and competent as I was, without a personal brand I was a nobody. Just another participant in another event on the calendar.

But with my rise on Youtube big changes started happening.

At an increasing frequency, I'd find top names dropping into my Facebook messages.

The first was a major player who kept a low profile but was making millions quietly in the background. He asked to be on my podcast and offered lots of support and praise for my brand in return. I didn't have a podcast but starting one with this singular episode was no issue.

Then there was someone I had met and got on very well with at a conference but only kept in distant contact with. He said he was seeing me all over his Youtube feed, gave me free lifetime access to his software tool and offered me an affiliate commission to promote it.

Another conference had an "apply to speak" form on their website which I had submitted multiple times and never heard a response from. I was a nobody. However, two years later I recognised one of my Youtube comments as the organiser of that conference, apparently a big fan. I was then given the big speaking slot I had tried years to achieve.

From that talk another invitation followed to speak in Las Vegas.

Perhaps the best example of these was a top gun in the SEO world who was at an intimate event of about 20 people. I tried to talk to them at the bar and they looked confused and flatly ignored me.

When they got on stage they apologized to the room that they were not a people person and therefore if they had avoided anyone in such a way, then this was common and nothing personal.

I later joined their coaching program at $200 per month to work more closely with them.

Fast forward a few months and they too dropped into my DMs saying they were loving my channel and wanted to join my own mastermind.

Conferences absolutely have their place.

Two years of them had many pros and cons for my business and lifestyle.

But Youtube was networking on steroids. Rather than traveling across the world to try and get some words in with a big name, they were now coming to me.

Everything I had painstakingly tried to build through in-person conversation, trying to be in the same room as them, suddenly flowed to me without leaving my house.

And when I did turn up at a conference, I was a legend. No more trying politely to get a moment with someone you had listened to for years, they already knew me and told me they loved my work.

I've gone from paying hundreds or even thousands to get in a room with the right people. Now the right people find me, and I need nothing more than my laptop and my phone camera to achieve that.

THE REAL MONEY

Many aspiring YouTubers obsess over fulfilling the requirements to get monetised. The fact is that these kinds of ad revenues are very poor.

Yes, there are plenty of professional YouTubers who make a huge amount of money this way through sheer volume.

But that is a long term grind and also very unpredictable. What we want to achieve is fast cashflow in just a few months with fewer than 10,000 subscribers. I've heard vloggers with millions of followers complain about being broke with pitiful ad revenue and then taking on product placements for just a couple hundred dollars.

Affiliate marketing is definitely a step in the right direction where you promote products for a commission. This is naturally very effective on YouTube has there is such a demand for "how-to" content.

But even then I have found that you have to sell a lot to make any real money out of this.

A far better approach is to zero-in on solving a specific problem for people with wealth.

Remember that the world has some very big discrepancies in wealth. Most people are, frankly, flat broke. But you don't need to go far to find plenty of people who have money to burn - supercars, super yachts, private jets.

I once met the huge digital marketing and SEO celebrity Neil Patel who mentioned he was trying to stick to a (very generous) monthly budget.

When I asked what his spending look liked before, he mentioned a time he was travelling with his family and his assistant. They went to and Indian restaurant and he found after that his jacket still carried the scent of the restaurant.

This is not an issue I've ever encountered before, but he said in this kind of situation he would send his assistant out to get another $4000 jacket and dispose of the old one.

If you have had a service business for any length of time you will surely have encountered the vast difference between two cohorts of clients: those who ask about the price, complain, negotiate and are never really satisfied, and those who give you the retail price willingly and don't quibble.

You don't need to serve 99% of your Youtube audience to make money. Just serve this 1% who see you, trust you and want you to solve their problems.

I've talked about how when my channel took off I was closing about six new clients a month from Youtube. That is obviously fantastic. But run the actual numbers and that is vanishingly small. My videos were getting about 40,000 views and 1000 subscribers per month.

And yet I was making more money than I ever had before, with less effort and barely any money spent.

Whatever industry you are in, your ideal customer profile should represent the top 1% of that audience.

Now I know what you're thinking - there are plenty of high-volume niches out there where perhaps you'd rather sell a lot of lower ticket products.

And that is indeed true.

For instance, with my SEO audience I was getting a lot of queries with a budget around $300, a long way from my minimum of $2000.

There was nothing hands-on and Done For You I could do for that price.

As a service business owner you really have to think like a doctor or lawyer. $500 - $1000 an hour on everything you do. That means if you have to write a few emails then you are already incurring significant cost.

By the time I have taken on a $300 client, done the work and paid for any specific deliverables and then emailed the client the finished work you are already at high risk of breaking this boundary.

At that price they are likely to come back with questions and concerns, which brings your hourly rate down significantly.

Eventually you'll find yourself constantly fighting fires and barely breaking even when you should be focusing on working on your business rather than in it - being the brand and growing your leads.

But there are of course more hands-free options and this can be a solution for lower ticket markets. Courses, memberships and other resources.

Now I would advise presenting these as a lower ticket option rather than the end goal.

Let's take the example of a gaming streamer. These guys get huge volumes of traffic. And the majority of that traffic is 12 year olds without a credit card.

But as someone who has found myself gaming more as an adult than a teenager, I know the pain of wanting to be able to pick up Call of Duty or Grand Theft Auto only to find I am up against those same 12 year olds with years of experience several hours a day.

That tells me there is definitely a top 1% who would be prepared to spend big on one on one coaching.

Now maybe a streamer has a course or a membership for a few hundred dollars. But this ideal client doesn't want that. They want the easy quick fix with the highest chances of results.

These are the people who buy the most expensive wine on the menu because its easier for them than risking a cheaper wine.

Think about business class on a flight. You get there just as fast with economy at a quarter of the price. But plenty of people prefer some space, better food and drinks and a chance for a lie down. And these tickets sell out. Even in times of economic hardship, it remains normal for luxury brands like Rolex and Bugatti to have a waiting list.

My point is simple. Rather than devaluing yourself with a $200 course or membership and nothing else, have something really special and expensive on the off chance that you have a few ballers in your audience.

You will have an easier life selling to a handful of these superfans than an army of more casual viewers.

Yes I get plenty of $300 queries. But I've also had clients sign up to $7000 per month over a 20 minute sales call after watching my videos.

(In editing this book a few months later I can now add we've had agencies buying from us at $20,000 per month)

Keep the lower ticket option, but a high ticket premium option makes this look cheaper by comparison.

Imagine one YouTuber you like has a $200 course and nothing else. Another has a $5000 VIP level and a $500 course. Which of these seems like they have better value to give?

The perceived value of a $500 sample of a $5000 product is much greater than the whole of a $200 where the ultimate ceiling remains $200.

Now I would recommend starting off with the premium option for the simple reason that it is so easy to set up. As soon as you get into courses and memberships the complexity increases even if your total addressable market also widens. The premium option is you. The surrounding technology is minimal. It's about your time and expertise.

The low ticket option becomes a more complicated case of how you package yourself into a self-serve option that's scalable across thousands of accounts and still offers value.

That said there are plenty of downfalls to running a service business in terms of team and processes and, worst of all, churn.

It took me a while to realise this and it only really hit home when I experienced it personally. If your average retention is say six months to a year, which is pretty standard, then you could have a record breaking month of sales in January, only to experience your biggest loss of revenue before the end of Summer.

This is the client treadmill. If you sell more plans then you have more clients dropping off the other end down the line. So you end up working just as hard to just stay at the same level. And if you're like most agencies, you'll be scraping by with a margin somewhere around 20 - 40 percent.

Imagine you've hit your wildest dreams of scaling an agency to $50,000 per month in revenue. But after the cost of deliverables and staff you're only left with $15,000 per month. If you've truly built a productised service with solid Standard Operating Procedures that makes you largely redundant apart from getting the leads from Youtube then that might be appealing.

But if, more likely, you're still just trying to build the thing and find yourself trying to run and improve the service while also hauling yourself on camera everyday trying to create great content, in an industry that may well not exist in 5 years time, you might look at your lawyer and management consultant employee friends with a degree of envy.

It is for this reason I quickly found myself working ever more towards high-margin info products like memberships, courses and even sponsored videos. We'll come onto these later. But I maintain that these are best left as a diversification down the line rather than your initial core offer.

TECHNICAL SET UP

Now I've given you a lot of talk on mindset and taking action. How do you actually do it? What delayed my YouTube success by years was equipment. And yes that was an excuse.

But it's true that so many people talk about starting Youtube and immediately get lost in the hunt for the right microphone, camera, tripod, ring light, soundproofing, studio space and more. The list is endless. And I agree that there are plenty of Youtubers whose videos look fantastic.

But we are playing a game here of speed and volume. I only got the results I did through posting daily and maintaining that. It took three weeks for it to yield a client so factor that into your expectations.

I've done the research a few times over and got caught in the trap of not wanting to invest too much in something that might not work out, but also not going cheap and ending up with an imperfect result.

But the answer really was to ignore it all.

If your laptop - and any other equipment you already own - is good enough for screenshares on Zoom then it's good enough for Youtube.

I started off with Loom as a simple screen share tool. It has its own basic editor within the browser version so I could see the waveform lines of audio and simply delete the blank spaces.

That was pretty much it.

I called this the 10 minute edit for obvious reasons. 10 minutes recording, 10 minutes editing and you're done. Download it and upload it to Youtube and it's on to thumbnails which we'll cover later.

I've found I can do about three recordings in one go before I start losing my touch. You'll have to work out your own cadence that works for you but I definitely recommend batching and doing several at the start of the week rather than one a day where you have to get in the mood, set up and then forget your microphone is off or some other technical fault that means you have to re-record.

The next innovation blew Loom out of the water. I had heard of Descript plenty of times for being able to edit videos by editing the text rather than dragging the slider all over the place. But I didn't think that justified the subscription cost when I already spend more than $1000 a month on a huge range of software thanks to many "it's only $30 a month" style decisions.

What I didn't realise were two incredible features that transformed my production speed and quality.

First is you can automatically remove blank spaces - so rather than fiddling with gaps on a timeline I can instantly set it to remove any gap of more than 0.3 seconds.

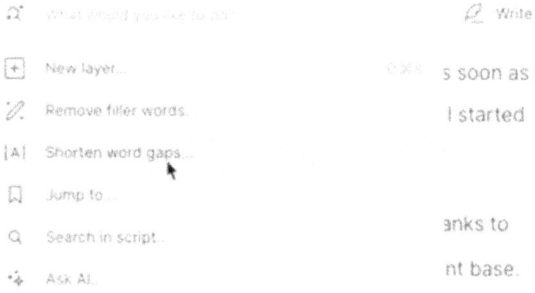

This makes for a much more engaging video in that choppy fast-paced style we've all grown accustomed to. This has a great side effect while recording that if you feel yourself losing your chain of thought or going off topic you can simply pause speaking, take a breath and then resume and the blank space will then be seamlessly removed.

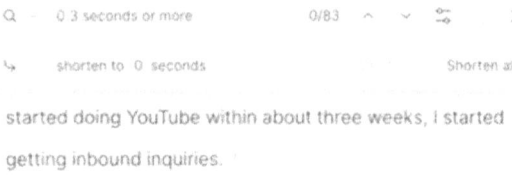

started doing YouTube within about three weeks, I started getting inbound inquiries.

At the time that totally saved my business, but thanks to alleged cancellations and the shrinkage in my client base.

I've sometimes stared at the camera for 30 seconds waiting to get my momentum back.

Then there's studio sound. Lots of people commit to a specific Youtube space with soundproofing and high end microphones. The Descript "studio sound" feature somehow uses AI to make your poor quality laptop microphone in your living room sound like a podcast studio.

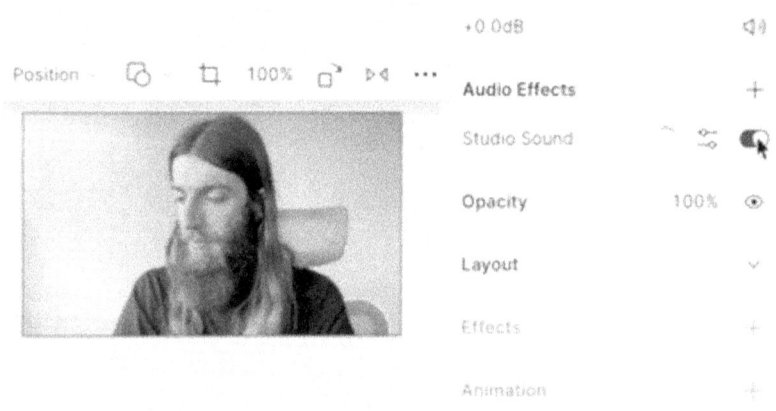

These are the two steps I take before exporting it directly to Youtube from within the Descript app. No need for lengthy downloads that take up your storage. Everything is saved on Descript's own cloud.

I say you can export directly from the Descript app but the truth of the matter is this is really buggy.

I've found you have to sign in and press the "export" button a number of times to get one successful upload, sometimes having to sign in again, and then delete all the duplicates that inevitably appear over the following few hours.

However, try to export manually and you'll find yourself waiting around 10 minutes or more and so I happily take the repeated hammering of the export button any day.

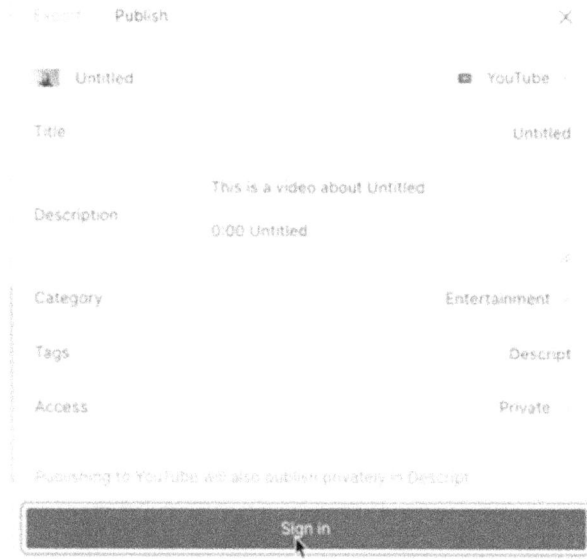

One other upgrade I made was using my iPhone camera connected by wire to my laptop and a ring light. But these are nice to haves rather than essentials.

If you do choose to go down this route then details depend on your platform. If you have a Mac and an iPhone then Apple has its own native feature that lets you use your iphone as a camera right out of the box.

For other setups you may benefit from an app called Camo which enables the same kind of setup for other platforms.

Camo also has its own production studio to play around with logos, spotlights, blurs and more so there are a lot of benefits to this for around $10 a month.

I challenge you to put down this book right now and record a simple screen share with your laptop.

VIDEO IDEAS

It is very easy to get to a point where you feel ready to start and then have no ideas for a good video.

I generally find this comes and goes. Sometimes I can think of 10 ideas for a video and other times any idea I come up with doesn't seem worth it.

It's usually right after recording that I feel the positive energy - mainly because it has taken me just 10 minutes to record a good video. Suddenly the barriers disappear and I realise any idea is valid because it takes just 10 minutes to do. I could record five videos my brain has dismissed as not good enough in an hour and then find one or two actually perform really well.

It's easy to forget that what seems obvious to you in your daily work could be revolutionary to someone else. If you're anything like me you've probably honed your expertise over many years and consumed a huge amount of content in that time.

You'll be surprised how often some simple concepts you thought everyone knew turn out to be game changing.

I met someone at a conference who was a legend in my industry. He had once done a case study where he got a new website earning $70,000 per month within six months of launch.

But while I may have been star struck he explained a particular issue he had been having, to which I gave what I thought was a solution everyone had heard about. He and his business partner looked at each other in amazement.

"That's a golden nugget," he said. Problem solved.

I have this same experience at just about every conference when watching the talks. An apparently big name can say some basic beginner stuff and then have a crowd of people around them afterwards.

So I encourage you to break down your regular activities and do a video on each one. We'll come onto hooks shortly where I'll explain how you take a mundane process and turn it into a powerful video title.

I definitely recommend a Youtube keyword research tool like TubeBuddy or VidIQ. These give you an idea of volume around a query and so you can quickly find out if one of your regular processes is actually a solution that people are searching for.

I'm not too guided by these as Youtube definitely rewards virality and so you can get a lot of views from a powerful video that doesn't address subjects with particularly high search volume, but they do help.

The key is embracing that volatility where one day you might have just one conversation or one train journey that sparks ten video ideas. All of these must be recorded somewhere so that as soon as you hit that wall of "I have nothing to talk about", you can review your notes and force yourself to try recording one or two of them, and then the rest will follow. Just like writer's block.

I used my simple Apple notes app for this on my phone. But as my team has improved from Virtual Assistants in the Philippines at $800 a month to A-player experts at $3000 a month, I've been migrating all this to a single Slack channel. This makes me the figurehead, more like a marionette. They can do more of the heavy lifting of ideation, editing and publishing while all I have to do is press record.

SCRIPTING

One of the most common questions I get about my Youtube process is scripting. Again lots of people are perfectionists. I happen to be rather chaotic.

But generally I follow the same principles as when I'm public speaking at an event. It's good to have an outline, but mostly you want to talk from the heart.

You are after all the expert on your subject.

I've watched nervous speakers recite from a script shaking in their hands and it is tragic. No matter how thorough and detailed I've been in my notes I will always leave them on the table, near enough for an emergency but far enough to no longer be a distraction.

Youtube is the same. I may well plan out the sequence in advance, usually opening the chrome tabs I want to demonstrate.

On sales calls prospects often praise this "hands-on" nature. They love the authenticity of watching me work live. Often I'm not even working but simply talking through a process - explaining how I would approach something even if I haven't actually done it.

There are times I've tried to take more of a talking-head style like some of my more established competitors but I quickly received criticism - my audience much prefers the direct demonstration.

Some people like to go for more of a webinar style and write out their points on a notes app in front of the viewer like a whiteboard.

People love diagrams and methodologies. You can get some attention by explaining your point well, but typically people get much more excited when you call it your special "Mastery Blueprint" and draw out some triangles - "specificity", "one-ness" - and any other corporate jargon you can come up with. Again I think this is just friction, but I have on occasion used Canva's whiteboard feature to illustrate a complex point.

Another great trick especially if your niche is more abstract is to present a slideshow. Again people love webinars. It's fancy packaging that turns something vague and intangible into an actual product - and you can do them for free on Youtube.

This is great if you worry you might skip over key points as well as giving you more to hide behind if you're shy, rather than your viewers watching your every cursor movement.

I'd still keep your face speaking in the frame though rather than doing pure screen share to maintain that instinctive connection and trust-building.

I've even tried instantly generating AI presentations with one of the many apps available on Google just to give myself a baseline.

In my case I wanted to talk about SEO for coaches but also wanted to target the broader marketing for coaches niche.

I generated a presentation in minutes, quickly breezed through the fundamentals of the other marketing channels the AI slideshow has recommended - adding in my own thoughts and tips where appropriate - and then went deep into explaining the SEO section far beyond what the AI had summarized and presented my call to action to download a PDF lead magnet and book a call.

Crucially I find the beginning and the ending are the hardest parts. For opening I will often hit record only to find myself lost for words. The trick is like a sniper to take a deep breath, and then pull the trigger.

I typically dive head-first into the topic. I have discovered X. By the end of this video you will be able to achieve Y. Recently there has been talk about this issue.

As for ending an intelligent person would have a series of calls to action - join my mailing list and receive this bonus, ask me any questions in the comments and please don't forget to like and subscribe.

I will quite often reach a natural conclusion and simply stop recording.

While I focus on keeping it simple and removing obstacles I would recommend some thought in the actual sequencing.

HOOK AND TITLE

Your hook is everything. It is universally documented that a video titled "How to achieve [dream outcome] with [trending topic] without actually doing any work" will vastly outperform anything deep and meaningful.

But we need to maintain that energy throughout the video while also delivering great content.

The first 30 seconds of the video is crucial as it seems this is where Youtube pays the most attention to ranking. If more of your viewers watch beyond 30 seconds then your video will get a huge boost.

To achieve that I recommend continuing the hype you started with the title. I just continue to sell the upcoming content of the video. Below is just a vague example of this.

"In this video I am going to show you how I achieved [dream outcome] without [friction 1], [friction 2], [friction 3]. I have tested this a number of times and it works really well. Many people make the mistake of thinking x but later on I'll prove to you why y is better. Make sure you watch to the end as I have one extra bonus for you."

Remember that people are more motivated by fear and avoidance of the bad than the attraction of the good, so you really want to sandwich them between their dream outcome with your method and the fatal mistakes they could make otherwise.

Now this might come across as sleazy marketing but you can make it your own. Remember that you owe these people nothing. They don't have to watch your video. I don't care if 50 people think I'm another sleazy salesperson if one person thinks I'm the answer to their problems.

Plus lots of us overestimate this risk. I've given talks where I've given a load of case studies and worried about being too pitchy, only for people to the approach me afterwards asking "Do you take clients?" Apparently I wasn't obvious enough and could have been far more commercial.

And that brings me to the next important part of the sequence which is your call to action.

CALL TO ACTION

I definitely got some great results with purely informational content where I would drop in case studies and references to clients with no calls to action. But forcing leads to Google me and contact me directly might have seemed great when the reality was I was probably missing out on a huge number of potential leads who didn't go to that length.

Now while I say you shouldn't be afraid of selling, it's fair that most of your audience and potential clients don't want to be pitched at the beginning of a video. Especially if they've already had a load of Youtube's ads.

But equally the pitch is really important. The fact is you really have to guide people to buy from you. If it's not obvious your expertise is available for hire you will be leaving a lot of money on the table.

This would be well placed at the end of the video except that the majority of your audience will have dropped off by then.

And speaking of audience, we may be talking about selling but we also want to grow our audience. Building that audience will help out not just your current business but all your future businesses. This is the beauty of personal branding. If you ascend from marketing guru to broader business guru, or lifestyle expert, it's very likely your first audience will still be interested in your later ventures. They are after all buying into you as a personality, not just what you're saying. A friend put it well when he said that people buy from people.

As I've said before, plenty of Youtubers will go from selling their own product to simply promoting someone else's, whether through a sponsorship deal or an affiliate commission. That saves them all the hassle of managing clients.

There's also no reason you can't open up additional income streams from your audience while still focusing on your core business. I make most of my money from clients but in all my tutorials I promote a number of software products I use and even other people's services when its a service I don't provide. These add up to a nice level of additional income which I share in greater detail in my Youtube Millionaire Mastery course.

Meanwhile, your audience is a compounding mechanism. You want to get maximum engagement on your videos to make them rank. There's no better way to do this than using your existing audience. You want to promote every video you publish to them.

I therefore recommend cultivating your audience very early on in the video. So after expanding on the hook and telling them what they will learn by the end of the video, I go into a hard sales pitch.

At this point they are primed to listen. They are excited for what comes next.

LEAD MAGNETS

The way you achieve all of this is with a classic lead magnet. In my case I offer an email newsletter that promises to go into further detail on advanced strategies. If I find a new resource that's sufficiently powerful I will often put it in the welcome email for this list, announce it in a video and tell my viewers to sign up to the email list in order to receive that resource.

You can also use classic lead magnets like downloads, courses and more. I've struggled for years to get people to sign up to lead magnets from blogs or ads but somehow the Youtube audience is much more eager. Some of these resources I demonstrate in the video and it wouldn't take much digging to find the resource without signing up, and yet those incentives work beautifully.

Throughout this book and your Youtube mission, remember this. People love gurus to follow. This is clear throughout history. Even though I like to think I am above reality TV and TikTok influencers, the fact is that even I have my celebrity role models who do have an incredible amount of influence over me. We love to have examples to model ourselves on. And we love to give responsibility for our decisions over to someone else.

When you are building your channel, you are very likely to start cultivating super fans who decide you really are their visionary. You have it all figured out. It's much easier to believe that than to face the harsh reality that, frankly, no one has the answers.

It's for that reason that a growing Youtube channel seems to carry an unreasonable amount of power.

So when I say to go and join my email list for an incentive that might not even be that revolutionary, I am shocked by the number of people who sign up.

I've tried to take this further by stacking value and adding lots of resources into that welcome email.

That means my call to action has become an extensive no brainer offer.

"[hook and promise of the video] BUT FIRST, don't forget to sign up to my Ranking Revelations newsletter where I share the tactics that I can't say publicly on Youtube. These are not repeated so you have to be on the list when they are sent. PLUS in the welcome email you will receive a host of other benefits including three free chapters from my book, my favourite tools to use and five of my top Standard Operating Procedure templates."

I can't overstate the importance of calling this out early in the video. If the majority of your viewers only watch the first 30 seconds then make sure that 30 seconds does everything to retain them for longer and get them into your funnel if they don't.

Everyone who signs up is then automatically put into a sequence of emails once a day that promote some of my older and most successful videos. This both encourages those videos to keep ranking on Youtube while also giving that audience more time with me and my brand, nurturing them towards a sale.

Every video I publish also gets promoted to them. We'll cover this later.

The important thing about lead magnets and any other action you want your audience to take is you must state it in the video, preferably early on.

Plenty of Youtubers simply put links in their description and hope people find it. When you watch Youtube videos how often do you check the description?

You have to tell your audience to get the lead magnet, and give them really good reasons for doing so.

Down the line you probably want to consider a custom lead magnet for each video. In my case all I have to do is add the latest resource to my welcome email.

I would avoid falling for the classic internet marketing cliches like free ebooks. I would look for a serious missing link your audience need to achieve something.

When I realised how well my channel was doing and how massively under-optimised it was I knew I had to get building an email list fast.

I had recently discovered a PR website that was getting serious traffic and anyone could place an article for just $75.

Most sites like this easily charge $500+ so this was a big opportunity no one was talking about.

I simply did a video case study on how I had placed an article on this site and was now getting some good traffic, while blurring out the site name.

I announced excitedly that this was a golden opportunity, but as I didn't want to ruin it for everyone by creating a rush that overloaded this website I would only reveal it in my newsletter.

I got about 300 signups in just 24 hours.

DESCRIPTIONS

Your YouTube video description doesn't serve a whole lot of purpose but there are some key things to include. If you are addressing particular keywords you know have volume, as proved by a tool like VidIQ, it is worth including these in the description and the tags.

The top of the description will also show on search results so make sure to do everything you can to encourage people to click on your video rather than a competitor.

To save time with my high velocity of daily publishing I tend to click the "view transcript" button once a video has fully uploaded and paste the whole transcript into ChatGPT and then I ask for a Youtube description that includes chapters.

Those timestamps that create chapters have a big benefit - they give you a bigger snippet just about wherever that video features on Youtube and Google search results. It is also strongly believed that they help videos rank higher on search.

I've got a custom ChatGPT prompt that will take my transcript and write me a description complete with chapters and then generate a relevant thumbnail.

The exact prompt behind this custom GPT is:

SEO Jesus Youtube Engine is designed for generating YouTube thumbnails, titles, and descriptions from video transcripts, now enhanced with DALL-E for visually compelling thumbnails.

It creates thumbnails with vibrant colors, suspenseful themes, featuring SEO Jesus. SEO Jesus has long brown hair, beard and blue eyes. These thumbnails aim to create an information gap and evoke emotions, using the brand color #FFA826.

All youtube thumbnails must include: an information gap (make the viewer question what happens next), trigger a negative emotion like panic, fear etc, and use a very big face to make it eye catching. also make the right size for a youtube thumbnail

Titles and descriptions are SEO optimized, with clickbait elements, chapter markers for viewer engagement, and include useful links. The engine adds these links to its descriptions:

1. Work with me: https://seojesus.com/apply/
2. Learn from me: https://seojesus.com/revelations/
3. Optimize your page: https://powerlevermethod.com/correlational-SEO-tools/
4. Fix site speed: https://powerlevermethod.com/speed-fixed/
5. Premium expired domain names: https://seojesus.com/premium-domains
6. Build automated links: https://stewartvickers.com/automation-offer/
7. Create AI content: https://stewartvickers.com/autoblogging-free

The engine then provides email subject line and teaser text. This should be a suggestive subject line that is again very clickbait promising very valuable gamechanging information that inspires the reader to open the email. The text of the email should then be brief and conversational, briefly suggesting what the video is about but not giving any secrets away. They should feel compelled to click the link and find out this new strategy.

Descriptions do make a good place to put all your links. However I would suggest avoiding this early in your channel.

Most social media platforms will reduce the reach of a post that contains a link. In fact when promoting videos on Linkedin, Twitter and Facebook I will avoid pasting the link directly and instead use a medium that typically gets the highest reach and engagement - an image of the thumbnail - and put the link in the comments.

These platforms are all about your attention and engagement. They therefore do not want to lose active users via an external link. It is logical that Youtube may behave in the same way.

As your channel grows I think you can start including your main links in the description as it's an easy process for you to tell people to go to the link in your description. In my case I tend to include my done for you application link, my newsletter and a list of affiliate links to tools I promote.

You can also try adding these in later after publishing and promoting when your video is already gaining traction.

THUMBNAILS

The perfect thumbnail is a constant fixation of aspiring Youtubers. We all know the classic shocked reaction photo.

From talking to some very respected experts on this they basically confirm that the cliche works.

When I first started on Youtube I borrowed a formula of a "reaction headshot" plus a visual element like a graph or a big arrow. I also like to include the keyword I'm looking to rank this video for in search, such as "SEO audit".

Since then I've been given some more advanced findings. One is to make the headshot really big, even to the extent of cutting off chins and hair.

You also want to create a "knowledge gap" which implies the hidden gem of this video makes the difference between success and failure. So you want the shocked expression and then something jarring.

This is quite difficult to do. I also found I was very quickly repeating the same photos.

So I then took these requirements and gave them to ChatGPT. From then on I could instantly paste my transcript and get a thumbnail that included all of these features, as well as my brand colours.

AI tends to get text wrong but you can correct this in a tool like Canva using the "magic text" feature.

Personally I leave these in because it all drives engagement - more curiosity and more comments telling me I've got it wrong which bump me up their respective algorithms on different social media platforms.

EMAILING YOUR LIST

One of the biggest mistakes entrepreneurs and marketers make is not growing a list. It takes an average of about five touch points to lead to a sale and those these are your hottest leads who are most likely to buy from you. It is also an audience you own, which is very rare.

Every platform has it's own "platform risk" where your traffic can change drastically. Many marketers will hail how a particular platform has transformed their business and then six months later that same strategy no longer works.

Organic Facebook pages used to be great but are now a mere fraction of what they once were. Youtube and Google are not immune to this. Owning your audience means you can hold on to what you have now for longer while also taking them with you to any future platforms you choose to focus on.

But the next mistake people make is not emailing their list. Whether through a lack of focus or, more commonly, fear of annoying people and driving unsubscribes plenty of people who take the step of growing a list and then not using it. Those leads go cold if they forget who you are.

I've read a lot of case studies that have confirmed you make a lot more money if you email every day, get a load of unsubscribes but also make a lot more sales.

It still pains me to send an email and see unsubscribe notifications come through. But it's just part of running a business. They weren't a qualified lead to begin with. No one wants a big unqualified list as they are ineffective, skew metrics and cost more to run. A small list of highly filtered leads is gold.

You can also include all kinds of triggers and automations to segment your subscribers based on their behaviour. Plenty will just be wanting your free offer. Others may be more interested in your content. Some will be qualified buyers.

I recommend publishing a new video every day if you can. I also recommend emailing this video to your list.

The benefits of this are significant. By getting your biggest fans to watch and engage with your video as soon as it is published you will maximise your impact on the Youtube algorithm. If your video looks immediately popular with good watch time and engagement then it is sure to reach a wider audience.

Meanwhile, you're enhancing your touchpoints. The subscriber who just stumbled across one video and joined your list is now given a daily update of more insights. Plenty won't care. But some will be hooked for hours - some of them will be your perfect clients.

I often have to watch what I say in a video as I know plenty of my clients watch every single one. My top videos tend to be shiny objects and hacks that get great engagement on Youtube, but truthfully to my clients with budget I recommend sticking with time-tested fundamentals.

For this reason we have automations set up so that as soon as someone becomes a client they are moved to a "clients" list and so we can make sure any emails they receive won't distract them from our core offering.

One mistake I see with marketing emails is making them to branded. You really want this to look like it came from a friend.

I use plain text emails, often my first name as the sender, and use merge tags to use the contact's name in the subject line.

Plain text is better for deliverability, but also looks a lot more convincing. I like just a few lines of copywriting rather than a big visual HTML email that looks like a brand's 46th one-off sale this year.

As for the actual copy, you really don't want to go into too much detail. You want to tantalise.

This email is not meant to give value. It is to drive the reader to click and watch the video.

I treat it as an extension of my headline.

"FIRSTNAME,
I achieved x with y without z. Here's how: LINK"

"FIRSTNAME,
Have you ever felt stuck repeating the same mistake when trying to achieve [dream outcome]? So was I until I discovered this powerful new secret. In this video I'm going to tell you exactly how I overcame [struggle] in just a few weeks. Most people won't take the time to learn and implement what I'm about to give you. The few who do will reap huge rewards."

ADVANCED ENGAGEMENT

Most people struggle to get any traction on Youtube. You publish a video and it gets 50 views. Share it on Facebook and maybe you get a few more.

To get more views you need more engagement which means a bigger audience in the first place through subscribers and your email list.

If you don't have these the grind can seem terrible.

Thankfully there are ways to jumpstart your progress.

Youtube is all about engagement but it doesn't care where that engagement comes from. Youtube is a global platform and so it fully expects videos to trend all over the world.

Just because your video is targeting a US audience doesn't mean it won't be of interest to someone in India. And as far as Youtube can see there's no reason why a lot of engagement from India is a red flag.

I get a lot of negative feedback on my channel that I use bot comments or fake comments. This is untrue.

These people are jumping to conclusions and assuming that what they can see represents my full process rather than just a fraction of it.

I actually leave these negative comments on my videos as it's all good for the algorithm - especially if they spark longer discussions underneath. How meta that manipulating comments leads to people commenting about my use of comments!

The fact is these suspicious comments are real people and not bots. They have real IP addresses with real user history. They are as robot as you or me.

And they're not just commenting. They are searching keywords, watching my videos - often multiple times - liking, commenting and subscribing.

I've since stopped the comments as my channel has grown and conversion has become more important than reach, but for a new channel I still recommend this kind of engagement whether you choose to include the comments or not.

Each time what Youtube sees is a video getting a whole load of engagement and watch time.

The exact balance and instructions of how to do this so effectively without causing issues is a secret held by VidOptima, a service I use for this complete package on every video.

They also include some actual bots that don't comment but watch the videos on repeat the full way through to the end, pushing my watch time right up beyond the average. These bots rotate their IP address every 30 minutes and so again Youtube just sees a mix of high engagement from unique users. Again the magic to making this work is in moderation to remain undetectable and yet still powerful.

Finally the video gets embedded on hundreds of websites in a page of relevant text. Again its not about the website itself or viewers discovering the embed, but Youtube seeing this video is so popular it has been embedded so many times.

This is meant to be a powerful decider in who gets to rank on the coveted Google video pack - that snippet of about three videos on page one of Google for certain searches. These typically get a lot of traffic over time.

The mechanics of sourcing a team of thousands of users around the world to perform this task is huge, and then giving the right prompting to get the best effect for each use case is another challenge. But I've had great results with VidOptima and highly recommend them.

Another option I'll cover later is the Youtube Promotions feature.

This is a fairly new black box that no one understands. Many of my colleagues are concerned about the quality of the traffic and I have definitely noticed the average watch time of any video I promote - probably the most important metric for Youtube rankings - drops through the floor.

However the sheet volume of traffic does seem to have a big impact with getting a video off the ground and popping up in places like the video pack on page one of Google.

SELLING TO YOUR LIST

Emailing your list regularly is one thing. But selling to it is an extra step many struggle to take. We're conditioned to avoid asking for things and so the idea of emailing someone a purely transactional email is scary.

And to be honest for the kind of service businesses I like, pure sales emails are not a great habit to get into.

When you're chasing $20 for an e-commerce product then sure it makes sense. Like how Amazon, eBay or hotel booking sites will chase you after you've looked at something.

But for the kind of service business I recommend we're typically talking more than $20,000 in customer lifetime value. These clients are unlikely to be hesitating on you because they got distracted and forgot. Usually, it's more about building trust.

Now the good news is emailing them fresh videos regularly will help to build that trust as they spend more and more hours watching you.

Crucially, every email contains a P.S. at the bottom. Copywriters have shown a P.S. tends to get a lot more attention than the rest of the email. The beauty of that is I can have a value driven email that builds credibility and trust, while adding the sales message at the bottom.

I'll generally tweak this to be relevant to the specific email so that it doesn't seem repetitive and anyone who reads a lot of the emails will see different selling points of the service.

"P.S. Does this technique seem too technical for you? We include it FREE for all our clients. Apply here to see if you're a fit"

"P.S. This is the exact process we use in house in our high quality agency service. Spaces are limited but you can reserve yours now."

"P.S. Effective implementation is the difference between success and failure. Don't think you'll manage it? Let us get it done for you."

What this allows you to do is cultivate scarcity. If you are on Youtube and email constantly selling then it often comes across as desperate. Clients know they can sign up whenever they like and maybe even get a discount.

This subtle sell in the P.S. means you can get right in front of your audience constantly promoting your service, but without a sense of pressure.

You can maintain a mystique of being oversubscribed and ultra-exclusive. This is largely truthful for a lot of businesses who would rather fill their limited capacity with a few high-paying high quality clients rather than selling to everyone at a discount rate and having a nightmare to manage.

You can also set up different triggers and automations so anyone who clicks on the apply now link gets tagged as a potential lead. You can then sell harder to them while keeping the broader list just for promoting your videos and driving traffic.

For lower ticket items like courses and memberships on the other hand you can definitely get more aggressive. A high ticket done for you offer should be premium and scarce whereas a course is much more of a one-to-many model. You've already done the work and your audience knows it doesn't cost you anymore to sell 1000 than 100.

That said you do need to work on overcoming hesitation. The course buyer with a budget of $300 is very different to the done for you client committing to a $20,000 investment.

We've all had those moments of seeing something we want and putting it off - you'll get it next pay check or once this other expense is out of the way.

Most of the time it just never happens.

This is common human nature when we know we can always get something. We usually want what we can't have.

Now one solution is flash sales. We see these all the time as consumers. But the danger is they devalue our product. People will get used to waiting for the next sale.

An alternative that works very well is using launches. There are plenty of gurus out there with lots of content on the perfect launch. The fundamental idea is quite simple: keep your course offer unavailable most of the time.

This takes some smart marketing as you need to build your list and then, rather than sending an automated email offering your course, you start manually priming them for your big course opening. You want to start building hype, so set a launch date and scale your volume of videos, emails and other content all building towards this launch.

When the date is ready you open the cart and keep sending emails about the benefits students will receive from this course, and announcing the sharp closure very soon. You'll probably make the most sales in the final few hours if you keep hammering the point that once the cart closes that is it and you don't know when you will be re-opening.

Course creators like this will typically launch a couple of times per year, each time raising the price. This gives them the power to not only say the cart is closing, but next time it opens the price will be higher. This has all the impact of a flash sale without devaluing the product.

In terms of payments there are some additional tricks you can include here.

One is a moneyback guarantee - there's a lot of legislation around cooling off periods and so you might as well make a feature of the money back guarantee to make it a no-brainer offer. Yes you will get some tyre-kickers who have a look around and then refund. But copywriter friends have told me the reduced uncertainty the guarantee gives buyers means you make far more money overall.

Then you have split-pay options. This basically allows you to take a $600 course and allow students to pay three instalments of $200. A lot of course platforms now include this feature.

When I came to launch my mastermind - two group calls per month which would be recorded and added to a content vault and a Slack community of members - I started by mentioning this was coming in videos and had a prelaunch waiting list on my site.

This went on for rather longer than I intended as I was distracted by the hassle of agency life. One month new high ticket leads were feeling very quiet. Fearing the worst, I knew it was time to get some cash elsewhere in a safer style. 50 members paying me a much smaller amount to turn up to two calls a month was exactly that, while cultivating a powerful network providing lots of value.

The prelaunch list had 50 people in it.

I chose to use Thrivecart to host the membership. Again its easy to get bogged down on which platform to go with, but Thrivecart was recommended by a friend and was a single lifetime payment. It was also very powerful.

I slammed together the sales page very quickly, an introductory video exciting members about what they could expect (one thing agency life teaches you is managing expectations and being clear about what is going to happen is essential), and a Slack channel.

I put the Slack channel invitation link everywhere. There was no way to automatically add people after payment. But I knew getting people into the active community would fill the time between calls with knowledge and value, as well as taking the emphasis off me.

I was going to charge premium for this. At $300 a month I knew that I could keep the mastermind intimate at say 50 members and still make $15,000 a month from it. But also I'd have a barrier to entry that meant that community would be full of A-players operating at a high level.

But to leverage the powers of urgency and the Fear of Missing Out, I emailed the prelaunch list with just 10 "super early bird" places at just $97 per month. These sold out within 24 hours.

And as a few "early bird" orders dripped in at $197 a month, we started getting plenty of emails begging to be let in at the $97.

Had I underpriced I could easily have sold out at $50 and then have people refusing to pay $70. With these kinds of products perceived value is everything.

VOLUME AND CONSISTENCY

I've referred to consistency throughout this book and with good reason. Persistence is the single biggest recommendation I make to people asking my advice on business and it's the same from my mentors.

Most people reading this book won't take action. Some may publish a few videos. If you make it to 100 videos in 3 months like I did then I will be seriously impressed.

The advice I've given in this book is all about doing the bare minimum. It is not about perfection. It is about relentless volume.

And I'm not just talking about publishing videos when I say persistence. Every step of this process is important. I've found myself slip on a single factor like call to action or promotion and every time the impact is noticeable.

If I do a video every day that has a powerful hook, encourages email opt-ins and gets promoted with a variety of strategies so it seriously trends then I make money.

I try and stay disciplined to do a video every day, but then I have to stay committed to making sure I give that video the best chance of performing.

A common piece of marketing wisdom is to stick with a single marketing channel until you hit 7 figures. Of course that can be bad advice if your chosen channel doesn't work. How you evaluate what works and what doesn't is often very difficult. But I've found that for my offer and audience Youtube is more than capable of taking me to beyond 7 figures. If you find the same then I encourage you to stick with it and not immediately attempt to diversify.

The idea of diversification is important but most people do it much too early before they've really hit velocity with what's working right now.

You're far more likely to hit seven figures and then have the resources to employ other channels if you start from this singular starting point.

Of course I'm not recommending you avoid social media altogether. Repurposing your videos for social media is a great way to get more mileage from the work you have already done and can all build more momentum on Youtube.

But if my method works for you I would avoid immediately reinvesting your newfound earnings into ad platforms. If anything I would probably work on improving your sales process and operations and creating an even better offer for your YouTube audience.

This is how you build a moat in business - making you harder to overtake. There's not much to stop your competitors starting their own Youtube channel, but you can beat them on sales process, operational efficiency and quality of service.

That's what a real business at scale looks like. It's not just getting more leads. It's converting more sales and then using your scale to lower costs and improve your margin. For me hiring a consultant underneath me was a big win. Despite wiping out a huge amount of my monthly profit until sales caught up, this meant I could actually step back from day to day operations. Which then meant more focus on Youtube and the big picture of the business.

MONETISATION

I've repeated that the easiest way to make money online is to launch a service business and promote it with a high volume of Youtube videos following my hook formula.

But needless to say there are many ways to monetise each and every video.

Many people get excited about hitting 1000 subscribers and getting monetised and yet this is vanishingly small money.

In the last six months I've made about $1500 in ad revenue.

I've made hundreds of thousands in my agency.

But once your core high ticket offering is running along nicely, preferably with a team of A-players to free you up to focus entirely on your Youtube presence, you can start to look at additional streams of income.

The beauty of this is you are already doing the work. It barely takes you any more time to include these moneymakers. You might in fact end up with more content ideas.

The first is classic affiliate marketing - promoting products with tracking links for a commission.

I've done this for years by ranking product reviews on Google. It's how I got into SEO.

But I much prefer the feeling of publishing a live product review that took me 30 minutes to record that instantly starts driving sales.

I make around $1000 a month in affiliate commission and its simply by listing the products I use in my description. Any time I use one on screen, I tell my audience to click the link below to get it for the best price or the right version.

I'll typically take my affiliate link with a long tracking ID and create a redirect on my website to turn it into a more compelling link like seojesus.com/writing-offer/. If that is too technical for you then feel free to use a simple shortening service like bit.ly. To me this not only looks better but saves someone simply searching the brand name or typing the URL directly when you've hinted that there's some kind of benefit to following your link.

This might seem a bit cheap, but the fact is review videos are some of the most popular content on Youtube. I've done product reviews which have not only proved extremely popular but have actually ranked on Google as videos. This is perfect evergreen content that will very often stay at the top of Youtube for months or even years to come, bring you more audience members and more commissions.

You can also drop all these affiliate links in emails to your list. My most common lead magnet that I use to encourage people to sign up to my mailing list is simply a long list of resources, many of which are affiliate links.

This was all going pretty well until an industry colleague reached out and asked if I had considered sponsorship.

A short phone call later and we agreed he would pay me $1000 a month to promote his service in four videos a month.

Now aside from integrity my chief concern was my seamless workflow. Would I be introducing more approval processes and holdups to my rapid publishing process? Like a return to the corporate website world of "can you make the button blue and change the heading back to how it was before I asked you to tweak it."

I sent him one unlisted video and he loved it.

Now $1000 a month was not a lot. At $250 a video that could take me half an hour to an hour to produce it was probably less profitable than selling consulting calls.

But the real benefit was the pricing point. Have you ever heard those Silicon Valley-style stories (or indeed the sitcom Silicon Valley) where a startup has no idea of its fundamental value - until an investor gives them a fixed amount for a set percentage of the business?

That is exactly what happened.

Next time I received an email asking for a sponsored video I gave them two options. A full promo for $1500 where I would sell them hard and email my list about them. Or a more casual mention in a video for $500.

This was an audacious pitch. But they took the $500.

I had doubled my sponsorship fee in a matter of weeks.

But then I received a direct message on Facebook from someone who claimed to have emailed but hadn't heard back.

I asked what their budget was - as I was having a Friday off with my partner that day in the countryside.

5000.

We had the call a few days later and she clarified that was the maximum budget and they were only paying that to a friend of mine who had 250,000 subscribers rather than my 8,000.

I stated 2000 and she seemed pleasantly surprised.

I had taken my sponsorship fee from 250, to 500, to 5000 within a couple of months. I hadn't even sent the first invoice when I closed this massive deal.

But I reiterate that this should not be strategy number 1. If I hadn't had a profitable agency in the background as my primary business I wouldn't have had that negotiation power. I'd be a shill, always looking for my next sponsorship deal with little real content in between.

However at $2000 a video as a theoretical price point things started to get interesting. This was an addition to my business, at no cost to my agency. It was basically more content to talk about, More authority to build. It was also

100% margin, unless you're a stickler and want to deduct $500 an hour of my director salary which makes it 75%.

I began to fantasise about how I might never have a stressful client exchange again, and just publish highly-paid videos.

Or even better. Hand off the agency even more to my A-player team while also getting more and more sponsorship.

That friend I mentioned who landed the $5000 deal was on a similar route, and was already making far more from his own e-commerce companies, speaking gigs and sponsorships than any remaining clients. He told me an incredible new strategy.

Youtube has a native "promotions" feature that people don't really talk about. They don't talk about it because you put $100 on it and you don't get any benefit from it.

I tried it on my most conversion-orientated video that goes step by step for 45 minutes on the whole process we use in the agency. Hormozi's "give away the knowledge and sell the execution" ploy.

I felt no benefit. And while I got subscribers from it they were about $1 each with no sign they were any better than organic subscribers.

Industry colleagues I discussed this with said they were concerned about affecting the metrics of the channel. You want Youtube to recognise the audience that likes you and keep promoting your channel to them, in theory, rather than just hammering your video at anyone who might click subscribe.

Everyone said the engagement and subscribers almost feel fake. But how on earth could Youtube get away with effectively selling fake engagement and subscribers on its platform?

But this friend was going hard on this. And when he explained why it all made sense.

Sponsors only care about your metrics.

Let's remember a lot of these people tend to be PR people. Smiley young and enthusiastic, recruited to try and schmooze top YouTubers into promoting their company.

They are not spreadsheet boffins obsessed with Return on Ad Spend and Cost per Lead.

My friend told me: it would cost him $20,000 to reach a million subscribers.

And in my SEO niche, that's huge. Most pretty large channels are only around 100,000.

I'd had direct experience of this whole game when I had that call with the sponsor paying him 5000. I had tried to steer the conversation towards that figure but she said "his following is much bigger".

He knew it was all about quantity, not quality.

Suddenly the idea of spending $20,000 to hit a million dubious subscribers seemed less like a naive vanity play and more like a Warren Buffet value investing thesis.

You spend $20,000 and people will start offering you near that amount just for one video.

Plus, if there was the slightest chance that some of those subscribers were reasonably engaged, then the benefit to my agency, channel and overall brand would rocket.

I realised to get those economics I had to stop targeting my ads to the developed world and open them up globally. Just like VidOptima's network of people around the world, Youtube doesn't care about geography and there are plenty of people in South Africa and India who are just as keen on my subject as those in the US.

You could de-risk this whole thing by making sure you only invested sponsorship fees into the ads so your "sponsorship empire" becomes it's own investment fund. Spend sponsor money to get more sponsors. Never agency money.

Once I had opened up my geographical targeting to the whole English-speaking world I had achieved a cost per subscriber of $0.046. Given my friend was already at 250,000 subscribers I realised most of the difference in budget to reach the million was simply that he had less far to go.

I also quickly realised how your hook just gets more important here. Some promoted videos just weren't hitting that magical $0.046 per subscriber price and I realised they were technical and boring in their headline. As soon as they were more sensational, but not so much as to trigger the Youtube ads restriction on clickbait, they hit that rock-bottom price.

I realised I could go further than reinvesting sponsor money.

Most of my videos will mention not just a few affiliate products, but simply resources with whom I have no affiliation. I like to praise good stuff when its deserved. How can I provide value to my viewers if I'm not telling them where to go and who to buy from?

I stared reaching out to some of them with whom I had a good relationship. I told them they were featured well in this video and, if they would like to put in some ad budget I would match it.

I got $300 from my first outreach.

Meanwhile my first sponsor had already mentioned about putting $200 on ad spend behind his videos in addition to the $1000 per month fee. I'd already blown that figuring out this process. So I gave him the same offer: "A few of us mentioned in this video are putting in $300 each and I will match it. Are you in?"

I raised $900 in ad spend, with only a third my own.

That video received 60,000 views and brought me 8000 subscribers.

Even better, as I started assessing how these videos were performing, I noticed I was hitting the top of Youtube with it and even sniping the Google video pack - which is often quite high on page one for certain queries.

The watch time on the promoted views was terrible. It brought the average view of the video down to 30 seconds instead of my usual five to seven minutes. I was therefore reasoning there would be little organic benefit to these views. Unlike a service like VidOptima that games YouTube into thinking everyone is watching your video extensively and therefore gets better virality.

But the fact these promoted videos were hitting these kind of spots - top of Youtube and Google - had to be a winner. I can only reason sheer volume of clicks was the answer here.

CLOSING THOUGHTS

I remain convinced Youtube is the fastest way to make money online and rapidly grow your profile- all thanks to its mix of wide reach for winning videos and then maximizing your time with those engaged viewers.

While I provide plenty of strategies for ranking videos and other fun tricks, the fundamentals are really very simple.

1. Publish a lot of content regularly. I still recommend daily. Keep your production really simple to enable huge volume instead of getting caught up in perfectionism. Done is better than perfect.

2. Sell your videos with powerful hooks and then deliver value once you have the viewer's attention.

3. Focus heavily on call to action to grow your list of loyal fans.

4. Offer a high ticket service or consulting calls. Then include other product offerings at different price points to meet more of your viewers where they're at.

5. With this kind of funnel it is very likely you will be able to scale your team and operations to a point where you can make yourself largely redundant from day to day operations and focus almost entirely on video production.

There is of course a level of risk here in that this is a business that is heavily dependent on you. While I envisage that you could stop publishing videos entirely and still receive some leads and revenue over months and years after, you can find yourself in a content treadmill you can never fully step off.

Videos on Youtube do have an evergreen element through ranking on both Youtube and Google but my biggest wins have always been the sensational viral topics - how I achieved x in less than 48 hours. These are not SEO-friendly keyword-based topics.

But with your brand established you should be able to develop other sources of traffic - a Facebook ad promoting a course from a big Youtube influencer is far more likely to succeed than one from an unknown entity.

Other bloggers and influencers are likely to be happy to promote your products for an affiliate commission for the same reason. As a big known entity your brand is an easy sell.

On the other hand you could also play the opposite. Keep publishing videos but focus on being the influencer. You can keep your services and products, or delegate even more of their running to your team, or simply let them die and focus on sponsorships.

White label agencies are a popular route I've known a good few influencers take where all they have to do is provide the leads.

The choice is yours. But I can confidently say that Youtube is the biggest lever I have ever pulled in my business. It has turned my personal brand into a real asset.

If I lost everything I have tomorrow - even my channel - I'm confident my footprint and exposure is now so big - even in my little niche of SEO - I would be ok.

If all my clients quit and other revenue streams broke down, I could just go out and sell on the back of my reputation.

Taking my $500 consulting calls down to a no-brainer $50 would be pretty painful but it would certainly drive a healthier income than a day job.

I owe it all to overcoming hesitation, embracing the fear and taking massive action.

www.ingramcontent.com/pod-product-compliance
Lightning Source LLC
Chambersburg PA
CBHW050236230526
45470CB00005B/1978